T0351442

WINNER OF THE BERKSHIRE PRIZE

"Load every rift of your subject with ore," wrote John Keats to P.B. Shelley just six months before his death. It's this line that I thought of again and again while reading Liz Countryman's capacious, ore-filled lines. Ore: a rock or sediment that can, with effort and skill, be treated, refined, forged into something of great value. The poet's ore is memory, or memory and thought, or memory, thought, sensation, and desire: all these elements are richly moving through nearly every moment of this astounding book.

Liz Countryman mines childhood for its longing, its intense sensations, its loneliness—a father's face at a drive-through, "a pile of tethered whipped-around balloons"—but she also stays resolutely in the present, finding there the parent's "soft anxiety," the perennial wish for stasis and movement at once. "I want everything to live," she confesses, and it's because of this desire that the poet is compelled to describe, to give life to the dead, to dig in the garden, to rub her hands across the wood of a table, to "shove my face into distance like a bouquet." This voracious relationship to the here and now presses firmly into and against the need to understand the past and all the longings it has deposited, like a residue of silt, on the skin.

I found myself so deeply moved by this tension, so awed by the intelligence that balances there between memory and present-time, that I frequently paused in my reading to at once note the world around me and to recall my own childhood—the precise scents, sights, and sounds of both. It was as if with this book, Elizabeth Countryman had granted me the gift of my own forgotten life.

FROM THE JUDGE'S CITATION BY JULIE CARR

GREEN ISLAND

GREEN ISLAND

POEMS

LIZ COUNTRYMAN

TUPELO PRESS
2024

Green Island
Copyright © 2024 Liz Countryman. All rights reserved.

ISBN-13: 978-1-961209-08-4 (paper)
Library of Congress Cataloging-in-Publication Data available upon request.

Cover and text design by adam bohannon.

First paperback edition June 2024

Tupelo Press
P.O. Box 1767
North Adams, Massachusetts 01247
(413) 664-9611 / Fax: (413) 664-9711
editor@tupelopress.org / www.tupelopress.org

Tupelo Press is an award-winning independent literary press that publishes fine fiction, non-fiction, and poetry in books that are a joy to hold as well as read. Tupelo Press is a registered 501(c)(3) nonprofit organization, and we rely on public support to carry out our mission of publishing extraordinary work that may be outside the realm of the large commercial publishers. Financial donations are welcome and are tax deductible.

I know, of course I know, I can enter no other place
—Oppen

CONTENTS

GREEN ISLAND

NARRATIVE POEM

I felt the authority of the arrangement:

how flowers with light behind them, hanging plants
near the phone in our house
framed that phone, the window,

our family dog chained in the shade of pines
and soft needles beyond the glass.

The phone like a faucet.
A little grime in its grooves.

In the morning, I felt a duty to keep—track of, grip

that house's side, that side's window
that led the nose toward brightness like a chain.

Not the story of how it was placed here, but all of it facing me at once,
a condition of my existence,
like someone gesturing and saying, "Here."

*

Upstairs, my mother's dresser like gates one swam through,
a ceramic awareness of several sisters

next to her, all of them including her, an awareness
that combed each day's uncertainty like a reef combs water.

The past stands still, upright, cheerful and the present
tries to ram through.

My past face's unresponsive confidence faces
my present face in the mirror, is unhelpful.

I was caught that day in the hallway
by the headmistress with a mouth of saltines;

every morning that week, I perceived a difference
between my feet on the orange brown carpet
and yesterday's hand on the brass handle of the pinkish door,
hallways becoming old thanks
to me, eroding them with my movement;

and keeping yesterday's grime, making me odd—
rubbed a wet finger on a desk covered in pen and whiteout.

*

Part of me is stationary and part of me passes through.
The stupid hair and the remembered hand.

A comb more memorable than the hair.

A bush, more memorable than air.

*

Now, to be 40 is to be a comb someone else's hair moves through.

I sense but can't describe some other, newer kind of openness
contorting me—

Now when I set the cereal boxes on the counter
when I make a shape out of them

what prior arrangement—what impulse disguised as practicality—
do I refute? And what *of* it
do I refute, and what of it do I carry forward?

What of that stubborn shape around me back then
do I now replicate, even as I refute it?

Or has one simply grown up from beneath the other
but stayed one thing

like the skin of a hand?

I have this statuette my mother must have given me
maybe on my First Communion—

a little girl in a pink nightgown
is pressed against an enormous hand,
snuggles in the cupped palm of this hand,
seemingly a man's, white, older (it is veined)—

the girl's face is old fashioned in its serenity. She has red lips.

The statuette suggested I was known
in ways both unknown to me

and known—hesitating,
how I was not like this girl,

the bare black trees outside my bedroom with the wind moving
   through—

a different kind of hand.

Wherever there is arrangement there is seeing, there is choice, there is
opinion.

I sat on the tar roof facing a June sunset
my fingers in the tar
in the dry rivers of the tar.

I thought about roads: an idea that was also real.

*

In my house, in this arrangement,
something about the twentieth century.

Not as a capped off thing, but forward movement
as I then knew it—a narrative.

Yesterday I ripped out the weeds in our vegetable bed
and I thought about the twentieth century.
I felt for the roots, slight but matted, and tore them up like carpet,

I felt them and they were cool

and they ripped more, the more I moved.

*

I think: I'll write about that yellow plastic grocery cart,
travel into memory

but then?
What do I do in memory?

I am an example.

I am the piggy who made his house out of sticks,
which will be taken off one by one by wind.

I remember when I felt pushed around by sex, a speck
bullied by my want for things—
roads and interactions

glances that weren't returned
a brick building that looked deliciously wet
moss delicious as the past—

and how my impulses secretly carried forward their inverse, an order
I spread into my life like spores.

Now I stiffen my hands, trying to stop something.

HOMEOWNER

Rather than a taut city of underground tunnels,

a land where everything is spread, everything apparent.

Trash slips from the street to the skin of a river

and the paths we drive and walk each day and the way we roll to and fro
on the bed

are an improvised sketch of what we most wanted.

As on a big beach one draws sand in a swath the width of two arms into
the space between one's breasts

this creation has razed large portions of the eastern seaboard and left in
its center a small, pointed mound.

The tunnels have been crushed and wetted, the contents of closets
minimized.

Two large banana spiders hang above our front door immobile on
fraying webs

and the sprawling municipality breathes all over itself, a conversation we
can't exit.

I sweep a lot of gripes around the floor,

thanking each Cheerio with trepidation.

This may be the epicenter of who I am—creator, tearing away the images of old bands I used to love,

letting go of cities, of infrastructure over water, of the vertical.

But I can't break the backyard to make better grass.

I want everything to live.

CAVE

That time we were in the cave
        in a small boat
a few people had jumped
        out already into
black waters going further
        into a cliff than
we could see the boat man
        un-shirted himself
dove and tugged our boat's
        rope slowly while
in the cave's mouth's
        outline on the surface
suddenly many bodies
        moving outward
struggling like they weren't
        actually moving
the light a golden
        frame around them
like an old painting holds out
        some gold thing
we don't feel much
        magnetized toward now
I felt a muscle of myself
        clench to stop the draining
of people from
        that time in the cave like
a gold frame very high and
        vertical almost
obscures the highest part
        of the picture we don't

dare look up to the sky
         also has a black mouth
and everyone's heads
         shrug upwards for air just
their necks and heads pulling like
         babies who go where they
are slowly tugged but
         also will themselves backward
to a soft dark they try
         not to see moving dutifully
toward the bright mouth

DRESSER

This dresser's wood has held some air in it—
a dresser of air—
and the air holds
something about what it was to be alive sixty years ago:
the kitchen brighter than its garbage,
the hanging kitchen ornaments almost sarcastically still against
the strength of the oncoming week
and how one usually looked at others in profile
over a jar of mayonnaise—

I am over you as you try to fall asleep in your pack and play, little
    Franny,
but it is hard for you because of your loose arms
picking up handfuls of damp sleep sack
and then dropping them, which wakes you up again.
The way a dresser holds

things that are "precious" but not exactly something you want to keep—
things that must be kept—
I am a repository

of your head smell,
some crumpled stickers,
an accumulated mass of scraps I can either
put in a box, glue down in some arbitrary order or throw away
so they'll sit someplace in my mind's landfill.

The dresser is both useful and imaginary.
I have my clothes in there. But it's also my mind's dresser,
so that there is a drawer in my hands, tough to move,

and also an entire dresser flying behind me in a stiff wind.
This big old dresser was in my childhood room.
It faces me squarely, the heaviest piece of furniture in the house.
Showing me my lovely fifteen-year-old lip gloss
it used to say, *Someday, you might be shiny.*

Or *calm down—you can sustain*
the feeling of being in a room.
Just look at the room you are: a young airy body in stupid old clothes.

It's aged, it smells, it might have lost weight.
I like how it looks and I like how I can see all its sides.

Now I'm reading to you, Franny and Olive,
a book about the peace of arctic animals.
A walrus and a narwhal and an Inuit girl
watch a beluga "singing."
They notice each other and pose next to each other—that's a metaphor.
As we face the book, I feel so adjacent to you.
Is tomorrow worse than today?
Your imaginations speed ahead of the bed we're on
and these animals are dragging behind;
I tied them there.

I'm teaching you to use toilet paper.
It was ripped from the Great Northern Forest.

This morning, Olive, we leave you in the schoolyard
and you don't know we are leaving,

and when we come back a few minutes later you are crying with your
    teacher,

the sky hanging heavily as I hope the sky will always do,
losing its breath, or its breath lost—
the way the inside of a mouth can simply keep things still in there—
that thick weather calming the traffic
before a storm, during which
I'll be between you and the sky like a strip of cloth.

By giving each of my daughters a sibling, I also give them
some other region they're next to but can't know,
evidence of the past, bits,
as though memory could be viewed from the outside.
As in: plastic "Easter grass," rotary telephones,
a carpeted stair for my elbows,

a round of trees outside the living room windows
through which I was associated with the road.

Everyplace I ever stepped seemed like some potential way to always be,
as though I might have stayed there—
a thing I didn't choose, but could keep
as an everlasting option—a mood—

like staying inside on a cloudy day, and wanting the living room to be
    quiet,
the white clouds, the ageing year,
maybe touching one or two keys on the piano,

an hour until I could eat lunch, which would even then be early,
the mood of a weekday when one is at home but not sick—
the holidays are coming, the house is empty,
my dad has gone out for one hour but I'm not sure how long that is.
I feel just fine if I keep my eyes facing the front of the house,
facing up through the tree branches
towards the street, a quiet street on a slope,
where sometimes a car will pass and mostly it's not my dad's car.

This is just one particular day, seeking its form.
There's no weather. There are no dates anymore, although
today is October 23, 2017.
There are no parents in the house.

Every time a car passed I thought:
that car is like or not like my mother's car, my father's car.
That car is a Volvo, but not brown.
That car is brown, but not a Volvo.

In the future, if I could visit it,
I might walk around a strange landscape and then come suddenly upon
a dresser that looks familiar
and inside it there is some knowable air.

I know I just met you, but I'll still be here
when only by comparison or there being something different makes it
     so—
I'll be some other option, an everlasting option,

just me today, imperfect, spent,
not quite a good joke, falling short by watching the same movie again
or by wanting to go inside when we're outside playing.
The temperatureless air nearby a truck or argument,
an empty house we wait for bees to come and live in.
As certainly as this evening I'll
"make" you something to eat,
I am beside you forever
like a mood.

I PROMISE TO BE HONEST

about nature and stuff
the breezes blustering bits but
sounds like fun words
elephants of words
bushes blustering elephants

bits in the air hitting us
bees banging the storm doors
give me the feeling of falsehood
just a little like
winning at something fun

winning really kicking ass
bright faces and days kicked between
dark days weekdays winter days
separate faucets busy
with the toothbrush

or reusing my magnetic mirror
in the dark blue locker's
stickered unclean
its lock stuck never exact
and I got no pictures to hang up

these houses belong
to these blocks where bushes
lean like this in the spring when
the weather leans like this
selling itself to new tenants

I feel a little silly around
these blustering houses
I feel fearless like
feeding you in the wind
with a pit in my pocket

THE END IS ALWAYS SUDDEN

Fumbling forward in an arrogant fog.

The sensation of tiredness—tingle smell of swallowed coffee in the nose

is tiny, like Captain Cook's ship picking the edge of Australia.

He and my nose are determined nits.

Something eternal's surely obscured—?

The mouth-covering submission of having a vagina

of looking at the sky and desiring another order,

or not desiring another order (to be delivered by Cook or by nose)

but understanding the ridiculous fear that animates the oppressor

so small in a big space.

The memory of my father at the drive-thru window of a McDonald's at night on I-87 north, his face lit and strained serious, is easy

to describe, whereas someone else's foam earphones,

or a soft anxiety that wants you to lie in it,

or the mountains at night, in a kind of feminine community and exclusion.

How tiny I wanted us to be

on our journey which was a centimeter of atlas.

How my commitment to disoriented wonderment obscured the physical
reality of what we passed—

alien antenna,

romance of high school names painted on a rock face.

It's over and I'm on the long end of its pendulum.

A great lie I had constructed and am still lamely buttressing.

How the farm at night was dark and cool showing us the real meaning
of a house.

How the Lord might have thrown us over the Pacific like acorns.

It is the motion I make when leaving you in your car seat, facing
backwards.

How your warm organs in my embrace withhold the undiscovered place
they constitute.

FOREST

That time we were in the forest we felt we had almost reached the forest.

Somewhere in the energetic forest we played croquet and somewhere gravel roads moved like slurping glaciers.

In the forest all the roads seemed to draw us forward even when they dipped uphill.

Beyond these glowing trees, a suggestion of blue lumps.

The forest glowed radically—a new place we couldn't see.

The trees here prevented us from seeing the mountains we knew hung close, covered by trees.

We didn't know, in that forest, if we were also on a kind of mountain, but we felt the earth moving below us, a large ball under a carpet.

It forced the flies and leaves and hawks and it withheld the thrushes.

I stood at one point in the forest and a thrush weeped over my head and you were elsewhere, moving downhill probably.

Something was in its heart, and we were nowhere near its heart.

All our thoughts about the forest were immediate and valid.

Although we felt the potential to become someone else in the forest, we stood firmly in the setting sun and that other self moved away from us like a lengthening shadow.

The light was a sort of tide. And the trees were a kind of reef, lessening the sun's force.

Roads led out of the forest making us feel bare and small.

Our wheels were reluctant to release the gravel but let me also note that the moving car did not actually touch the forest.

It was as though the forest moved past us like a lover we were leaving at the train station, and we were on the train.

Ever notice some train stations make you feel you're already in the past?

Energetic forest like a grand old train station with its roof ripped off, full of birds.

We waited in it with a little dread.

What we discovered in the forest pertained to us.

A deer looked at us. The paths were mostly vacant. They were light. They meandered. They were obscure.

Nothing in the forest actually touches, or its small touches startle.

It holds many creatures apart from one another and suggests to each the presence of the others.

We cannot list them.

The flies are very big; they bite, even when you're riding a bicycle.

The birds have some warm and cold symbol in their voices.

They have some echo that makes you think you're listening to another moment in time. And there is the bird right there, high above where you sit.

The hawks suddenly look at us, flying their eyes directly into our eyes, swooping low toward our foreheads in the clearing.

Now we are remembering.

Wherever the woods carried the noise of a stream they also carried the idle noise of gunshots.

We were grateful for the actual meanings of words even when their structures branched beyond our sight.

The forest's way of obscuring so much gave us faith in what it held.

Or the forest's way of holding so much gave us faith in what it obscured.

It was never a matter of reaching the forest. It was a question of being invited in, and then of staying long enough that eventually when leaving it we might have the illusion that our car wound slowly, as though pushing against a rubber band, when really it must have whooshed through the trees toward adjacent forests.

Because of that forest—*our* forest—we were haunted by these other forests, which surely had their own sexy and dangerous dynamics.

The other, outer forests would surely have required that we commit ourselves to them, losing the first forest and entering some alternate one.

So we drove past them with our eyes forward, as if through a dangerous neighborhood.

And later when the highways led us to the edges of medium cities wedged into hills, we felt the way forests persisted, brutally injured.

Enormous, absent, alert forests where now a parking lot allowed us to rest as trucks roared through the intersection.

The intersection was on a slope. Here and there were trees. There was a lot of noise.

But some invisible forest still brandished its aggressive care.

Its demands were real.

We felt as though that original, far forest had been a husband.

It knew us more than we knew it. We could still feel its treacherous eyes. We were small and bent forward, moving toward where we headed.

Its voice, like a thrush's, seemed, even then, always someplace else.

So that we cannot expiate ourselves by speaking.

We can't exactly meet in there, but we dot the forest.

It keeps us awake, thinking of that forest heart. Sometimes we see the forest that one large suburban tree makes, holding things apart and hiding them.

It keeps us awake, knowing that roads extend from where we are, connecting eventually with those legendary roads.

CIRCULAR

Thank goodness waking drew a circle around that fantasy

Our kiss like two manatees bumping in gentle fear of motorboats

It was good to be on the bed's pink zone and the sun shaking at the window

Today's beautiful shaking draws a circle around that bed

I'm in the backyard, roots reaching toward their maximum scope beneath me

A crow cry's a jagged sphere bounding around my life

Aware like a control tower and me corresponded to it, glued to its map

Playing with pockets of space in my garden gloves and remembering in pockets

I have a taste in my throat and my throat is a hall

Where chairs have been dragged for a piano recital I'll fuck up at in 1987

My uterus is a snow globe where I can see a cornfield I drove past once near Easton, MD

And inside my lungs is a bad picnic, a total waste of time

My lungs push that picnic into a light cloud around me

Those pasta salads, that picnic-wish to be encircled

The succulent night makes a circle around the dry day

A book in my hand white on the pink blanket

With a whale filling it, with a room around the whale

Cartoon children pointed at extinct lizards

The deer lamp dug a sphere out of the absurd dark

What a relief to have escaped the circle to which a deer's hooves are glued

Where trees outside shuffled, old people moving

Around food coloring-flavored cookies in an echoing hall

And to be at this unfinished picnic

With today's trees at the perimeter of our yard looking like ambitions about mountains

The future a circle stepping away from them

Like my father walked backwards in the ocean when I could almost swim

I can see your real arms as edges of a beautiful lake cut

Vividly into my memory for a few years anyway

And holding you is like a pitchfork, is like a crescent of strings

As music goes, exploding from a single point

Holding you is like feeling wind blow dirt off me speck by speck

*

A CLEARING

Birds, we've cleared away your space.

The blanket of clouds has burned, leaving us bare.

A hummingbird sneaks into the yard like a ball of dust.

When a space opened, it felt like meeting a thing.

My eyesight suddenly better and the distance coming toward me.

I have wanted to shove my face into distance like a bouquet.

Like my daughter, playing with her doll house, tries to "go in there."

I remember stairs, wallpaper, poinsettias, mirrors, gates—

how we felt a big open weight that made the coins shine in your dish,

made Alex Trebek shinier in his blue square.

How for years everything felt quite new.

I shaved off a patch of my arm hair and was a little terrified.

One time, you opened the moon roof for me to better see

a mountain I pretended was above us

as our car ascended an actual, modest mountain.

That dark, softish plane retracted revealing a rectangle of ambiguous sky.

We drove higher up until finally we could see

a lot of land, so much

it made me feel embarrassed—how little of it I could identify.

I was young.

I couldn't look down from a mountain and think: *that's somewhere I've been.*

From in here, my skin felt smooth, but on the outside it had hair.

When I remember that unmade clay feeling

I want to say *I am she*

but pressing her to me, I feel a space, like something it feels good to squish,

a space pressed closer in and never getting, like a kiss.

I stare at what's apparently farthest.

A Friday dusk, tacos, asphalt,

the sun hitting each piece of gravel and each piece casting its shadow sideways.

The upstairs apartment of a friend now dead,

its sun porch and spider plants,

the immense landmass moving under us like a pool float.

When I remember him, the sweet feeling of simply expecting to see him—

to get up and get dressed and be a part of the dusk—

that feeling's like this space he's left.

(Instead of laughing at a joke, he used to look at me with conspiratorial knowing

so that I kept expecting laughter to arrive.)

One time camping, we came upon a clearing.

The woods darkened behind us but we looked out into an opening

that was like some book that you own and pick up occasionally but haven't read.

The sky, grass, water, trees, arranged as a hole—we camped there,

but the composite view distracted us from what was in our hands.

The pond: simple, unapproachable, sunken, pointed.

The moon, winking above us: *You haven't, like, escaped.*

I've felt like one (a clearing).

I've felt so unfamiliar that I've been sort of shy about saying *I am she.*

But maybe I pretend I can look at that day as one soft object

while here, the stuff that touches me

is sharp, antagonistic, countless.

Is the past big and soft, something I can press my face into, like treed mountains?

Or does it darken behind me—the awareness of that forest

as I dutifully faced a clearing?

In my memory, I never looked into the woods. The clearing was

hospitable and strange. It had been there a long time.

I was new.

Things I used to expect still seem to be coming up: I'm still expecting them.

So that remembering makes me wary and alert.

I remember one time at a party for a wedding—

the lake, blazing in the sun, seemed to charge toward us like a row of men.

My childhood, I realized, was rougher and windier than I'd assumed.

Here it was, coming to conquer me.

Let me describe the feeling I have about my family but let me not say that I have it

as one pays to have a view.

It's what, instead, I didn't achieve—

light blue water behind dark tree trunks, or a pineapple sign in a field of pineapples.

I don't know where those things were;

even then, I couldn't make them out

but I had the feeling, as I looked from the backseat, of having arrived.

When my first daughter was born, the yard seemed strangely open and wavy.

We sat on the porch.

I looked at some trees near the back fence and noticed how I didn't really know them,

imagined how long they'd been there.

Her head was exposed to air. The fall air starting to cool.

I pictured her future: lying on a bed listening to music, sun coming in the windows,

not much furniture, her own place. An aqua tank top.

The idea of moving somewhere far away swelling up inside her like a plant.

I recognized the room: it was an image of my own past.

My own mom had moved a long way from her childhood home.

I've often daydreamed about that departing ship, with streamers,

pushed out of the port by a kind of romantic mania.

In my head I see a colorful map.

But these trees at the edge of my yard were something else.

Absorbing, defiantly, change.

Their relative stillness as muscular in the uncertain air.

We were standing on the beach, watching pelicans.

I felt something almost like delight—

like an invitation to confess

but if confession might have been, instead, a space.

I was expecting something to approach.

Hot water, the bare invisibly polluted air between here and that ship,

as you and I stood, making a wall,

absorptive, like a joke not spoken or like air

a cave holds in.

That cool, desirous breath might be its own end.

The saddest thing, when someone's gone, is land.

No amount of accuracy will bring what I see closer.

Its arms seem open but it keeps receding as I move.

Remember when we used to go to baseball games, how we came out of the tunnel

and felt a dizzy joy—how sharply we could see so much.

In my souvenir program, I was hungry for detail.

Thousands of people, some patches of people in the same t shirt,

the flags, the direction of the breeze, the train moving past on its own schedule—

patterns, patterns, which today seem only like a composite.

What did a day like that feel like?

It must have been like reading, together, the same text,

but a text that seemed also to know us.

Then we moved along the highway after the game, west into the dusk,

the cars and their eyes lighting up, the idea that they held people less and less possible.

And later, from our house—all those planes waiting in line to land.

Cars moved past—I could hear them through the trees

always sounding purposeful

always moving toward the peak of some gorgeous bridge.

Even then I erased their variation

in my desire to be lifted.

This feeling of departure is a beginning we couldn't anticipate.

Permanent bareness, a clearing without precedent.

A long time ago, in the neighbor's yard, beyond the fence,

there were caged bunnies I couldn't quite see.

In flecks and pieces, past the dark mess of bushes, another yard opened—

the fantasy of a clearing.

I heard the manhole covers clink at the edge of block.

You're not here today. Birds are answering each other.

I hear them through three different windows so I become where they echo.

*

ERASURE POEM

What's visible is the remainder after an artful act of removing.
Clover, scrunched on the ground, still has height.
If you comb your fingers through the complicated stems,
if you kiss the clover secretly, the way one might kiss water while
    swimming.
The flowers look far away, they look like something I've said goodbye to.
Their smell is so fucking faint, so fucking gentle.
When they look at me, they might as well be shaped
like some family eye, a rib eye, a thick circular outline,
a logo one wants to eviscerate.
A whiff of duty. Praying on your knees secretly,
the way one might kiss the inside of a turtleneck.
Thank god the lawn is clear so we can stomp across, for we are in a
    hurry.
Everything wonderful and winking is shitty.
The flowers are just victims, one thinks, without sentience.
But having been so repeatable, having repeated all over the seaboard,
the clovers intimate with so many furred abdomens,
they are like grandparents, or, further, to kiss them
is like entering a regular day in the past
that is no more and no less than this.
Only that we're blindly held here—there are the clover blossoms.
Even a cow's gratitude, in a field of clover, must be mostly blind,
mostly nose. So many people died. And cows. The dead people
I'm thinking of now—seem to stare at me in a line.
They're Americans. They spread and spread this.
They're so dour with their seeds. They want nothing from me.
Can we have breakfast, can I ask you a question?

I remember my own past like I look at a Rothko in a traveling show,
    behind glass.
I can't see what I see, so I give up. We went by
the old ice cream stand and occasional Christmas tree place
to suck "grape" ices through a straw. The lawn called as if of old.
But we couldn't lie there—it was thinning, really, full of holes.
We had to stay where we looked at it obliquely,
our oblique look filling in the grass.
I guess we were also in the sun. Breathing gas.
Thinking about outfits and mistakes, and transgressions in underpants.
Some days feeling the permanent loss of what I had not yet even named,
rejecting and partaking in the contemporary,
watching a wide wash of birds fleeing like guppies.
I am drawn into the past, into rooms whose stuff I want to touch and
    name,
being in rooms like kissing something,
listening to the outside, the fair rides screaming in the night,
the breath of the house escaping into the night slightly, a hum,
the tick of the digital clock radio, a stick scrape.
Or else seeing a cold face entering my house—just the face,
although I know there must have been a bicycle and stairs.
I know it was December. The world felt like Friday or a harmful Tuesday
    morning.
I felt this slight sweating on me and I smelled a grill.
I had news in my pants. I wanted to be taken for a ride.
My memories of rooms are of the outside.

Pencil in the hot grass? I will leave you there forever.
I'm embarrassed by the nudity of my yard.
Or how on the broad quad, pen stuck in a page,

I must have felt protected by the date.
Stiff out there, phoneless, always dangling in public like a sign
or writing some name in red pen on a leaf
then rubbing it juicy, flicking it into the grassy bowl beneath.
Today I think I smell my daughter's head, but it's her teacher's perfume.
Something grows sideways instead of up—
an ambiance, my sense of the past that was, even then,
an assumption about the quality of a chunk of earth.
Whatever leafs, whatever animals I didn't see
made being there whatever it was.
I am trying to blow out a space for something to grow vertically.
When I move my hand, images come along as grudgingly
as teenage me on a hike. Handwriting in the wrong clothes.
I saw rocks, roots, feet, but more than seeing I felt
that the world was a humid Thursday
and the year a sneaker jammed stuck in a crevasse,
whichever year it was. As if someone watched us
with disdain or love, a kiss that didn't happen.
As if a famous poet passed by our restaurant on a bus, threw us a flower.
I wanted a lot of stuff, not that I can see it now.
What I wanted, like a large landmass, matters.

GREEN ISLAND

My father, wearing sneakers in the water

or maybe another man, some tourist, far off in the water wearing sneakers

(*that's what they do, the coral's so sharp*)

ticks from spot to spot, and the sea

seems to be heading someplace else

I am on the shore or my toes touch the water

or I have been walking out a long time and my sneakers are soaked and still the man is farther out than me

or I'm looking at him from the water, with the island behind him, turning its back on the sea

The scene, like a cow in a field, seems to walk away without moving its legs

Where is the reef? It's out for a stroll

Suddenly our feet are very dry

Under a bush is a cool dirt patch I stir with a finger

Inside the yellow windows my aunt and mother make dinner

The softest dirt, almost grainless

I will not have time to really go under this bush, but even as I stand here
I'm hesitating

Even as I stand here I've had a bath, my hair has been washed, in the
dark someone has been singing to me

and inside the suitcase on the closet's high shelf are a few particles of
sand

and on my father's soft blue Green Island t shirt

is a velvety white sun, a boat and capital letters

as he sits on a lawn chair in the evening in our backyard

by the house, where the island ends its day

through our hands, as they lose shape

as a seething point, like a star.

LEAVE

We were far from home,
we looked into each other's eyes and recounted:
we were far from home.
We were far in a house, in a boat, by a pile of tethered, whipped-around
    balloons
where we looked into each other's eyes and out
toward the road at night, or the ocean during the day, or the gray-brown
    buildings
whipped around in the sun.
Clover blossoms with their pale, compacted petals
cowered in the shadow of a crazy, governmental building.
As we counted the swarm of gravestones next to the Parkway, holding
    our breath,
we were gravestones in motion, gravestones
running along the side of a car like water a canoer's hand dips into
    casually.
The water that is the climax of a summer vacation,
the water that is the point of the vacation,
the contact with water that makes us feel,
in a far off place, assuredly ourselves.
Dark waters came up beside us and into our eyes—
we've remembered it over and over.
The water practically drank us, not the other way.
The water drank us up and made it dark.

The water drank us up and made it dark.
The water practically drank us, not the other way.
We've remembered it over and over:
dark waters came up beside us and into our eyes.
In a far off place, assuredly ourselves.

The contact with water that makes us feel
the water: that is the point of the vacation,
the water that is the climax of a summer vacation.
Running along the side of a car like water a canoer's hand dips into
   casually,
we were gravestones in motion, gravestones
as we counted the swarm of gravestones next to the Parkway, holding
   our breath,
cowered in the shadow of a crazy, governmental building.
Clover blossoms with their pale, compacted petals
whipped around in the sun
toward the road at night, or the ocean during the day, or the gray-brown
   buildings
where we looked into each other's eyes and out—
we were far in a house, in a boat, by a pile of tethered, whipped-around
   balloons.
We were far from home,
we looked into each other's eyes and recounted:
we were far from home.

SQUARE THOUGHT

Back there some tamped down ironic lust, pedaling,
and here, a corporate monolith and weeds.
From here, I remember that early afternoon in bed—headphones, sun—
alone, I made an avenue whose greens
moved evenly above my bike, like I sailed inside a tube.

A field of what I felt—I hoped—of others.
The big rock sunk in clay past the edge of the dock,
my white foot struggling up its slime.
And colored magnets slid on a safe, peaceful fridge.
If something slid me then, I still slide.

I remember that simply sitting on a boat, the boat
nodding wildly, felt like reckless sitting
I barely had the knack for. Music in my ears made space
that thrashing assent thrashed against. How
a tree breathes. How extensively a bird sticks out its breast.

When my trees were knocked down it was a development.
When my ribs knocked, trees grew among them.
I grew a forest in me to thrash against, thanks
to beautiful people's disregard in drab rooms,
next to sliding glass doors—forests of hands briefly circling me in dance.

My own body? It was a plane. It had a swing
and a rivulet, but it was something one strides across,
away from a tour bus, toward the edge of sea cliffs. A story flaps
between that past and where I sit. I made such
a square, the kind you don't reach the edges of.

TO AN OLD HERO

In my dream of you
you are a form of me
but you still seem to ignore me in your magnetic wisdom

You travel in crowds
you see over the bar
your eyes are hidden in your fantastic hair

The dark lane with dark grass
and train tracks and a dilapidated shed, now a restaurant
a place I never anticipated

is where I see you
busy talking to people and moving
from one station to another

I'm dawdling
Where will I spend my evening
Here are a few people I can try to talk to

Although there are a few people here
who even are they
When you leave

there's no place for me to rest
I will try to call a car
I can't see over the votive candles on the bar or pay my bill

In my memory of you
which is not a memory

I am in a room with you, of yours

filled by soft lamplight during the day
You are looking upwards and speaking
like a dad spraying a hose into the air

above his giggling daughter
As you speak and as I speak back
I have this road in mind

Headlights from a few hundred yards away
looking at me or not
and the curve of hills which now seem

like cupped human hands
dividing wet sand into roads
I had it in my mind

as you were speaking
A road I wanted you to see
in my hands, in my lap

next to the photograph of yourself with younger hair
that didn't look at me
My hands must have touched each other

YOU ARE IN A LAKE

Feeling like you're in the middle of it.
A small crowd of people you know
sits on a rock over there.
Below you, cold
waters like a monster's back.
The lake's skin
slices you up and down,
laps the burning air.

You feel as though you aren't in your own skin.
Or as though the whole lake were a metaphor
for the distant ring your life
makes around you, some faces at the perimeter.
Maybe a face looks at you.
Maybe many faces turn toward each other
and their laughter hurts your ears.
Flies, big ones, bite your ears
all the more when you go under
and come up juicy. Hot
flies. You are marginal,
hungry for dinner.
A loose pop reaches the crowd
and the forest behind them,
is delayed somewhere,

snaps them out of their talking,
a shot.
They respond
with a slight noise—

a grey sound they make,
many tiny things together.

When you were little
you were somewhere like this.
The hills were at that distance,
the people and trees
beyond you.
You were in a bathtub
or you sat in a yellowed baby pool
and bees gathered by a ladder.
The sky was past you
as a rule.

Behind you was
some original moment. Black trees
brushing a bedroom. A wooden kitchen
lit by music whose sentiment
you felt but couldn't identify.
Before you was a faucet of information,
books, television, wide
clouds.

At best, I'm this afloat.
But one can't write staring upward
through trees at dusk since
ink goes down
and they're over you,
attentive and distant,
like injured parents.

Or potentially they are different this evening.
The trees are real and withering.
I am in a hammock.
Some water falls in tiny
pieces in the hot forest.

ENVELOPE

There are camellia flowers
on the camellia bushes
the oregano is flourishing
sunlight moves on the gray wall
and shows the dust
on the window screens
a paper bag leans against
the side of the window
some of the leaves are green
and some are yellow
some of the trees are bare
some vines grow high
in the tall bare trees
old crepe myrtles
with bulbous blight on them
some of the leaves shimmer

Some of what I see seems to move
some of it seems to be still
some of my fingers move
when a breeze arrives the leaves
trying to be turned
the purposeful bend
in branches the purpose
no longer apparent
also leaves room
for the next thing

Some trash floated across a plaza
on a Christmas evening

in a show I watched
set in Chicago in the 1990s
George Clooney held
his wool overcoat around him as
discarded wrappers
pulsed around him like sea waves
other people crossed the plaza
and the camera lifted quite high
different kinds of coats
the plaza lightened with flying papers
some kids with bright
puffy coats
some adults with dark wool coats
he made his way across the street
his heartbreak seemingly
one more floating paper

There was an awful amount
of room around Clooney
remember that moment where paper
pulsed inside us like
we were full of imperfect air
that time a girl
who'd been nice to me
suddenly wasn't
and it felt as though a bush had been
ripped up from my heart
so that behind it I could suddenly see
another area

that had apparently been there all along
and I wandered in

Like a piece of paper George Clooney
may find new use
flying into different hands
I'm looking at you from here
with the camera and years after
I'm still concerned that you're cold
your coat still holds
reality to be coaxed out
a store
today
inert human designs
stupid purchases made in hope
routines that feel both awful and good
are all areas
like a swirling plaza
pockets of communion and pause
toys everywhere
books everywhere
and when we used to purchase CDs
here is your Christmas present
a little room for you to dream in

The decisions about shape
a tree has made
seeking and avoiding
leave room for light
I feel a small amount of room

balloon
a neighbor who dressed as Santa
opened his hatchback
on my block
for all of us kids
or everyone else
when I brought home the small
plastic helmet
an ice cream dish
how an awareness of
everyone else
was wound up
in my happiness

Someone is going to listen to you
90s Clooney
someone may still listen to you
the cardboard coasters
in bars
how they mop up
spilled water on the bar
the overpass
how my daughter
proclaims it a bridge
what is exchanged among people
almost purposefully
like a paper loose from the hand

A letter and an envelope
what I thought and

how it didn't think of me
as it moved around the country
in other people's hands
the afternoon was gone
but the letter kept it
in store
endless as a college campus quad
hopeless as a bird
on a quad whose hope
is emptied by the sloped quad's
tunnel of wind

Sometimes warmth feels so
slightly wonderful it is
extremely wonderful
December-colored grass and
chimes somewhere
movement somewhere
chirping
the tearing away of cars
a block or two from here
wind and cars sort of the same
the benevolent warmth
skin-thick warmth
browning of leaves
unreachable as the past
it is indeed the past
where I dream of you and find you
or hear your cries
in the driveway and anticipate you

hear the beep of the car as you lock it
shouts waving past me
like distant cars

We have somewhere to go
we can't linger here
we can't reach what is here
it's just like the past
that steady
that enormous
that familiar and unfamiliar
the gracious sun
unsettles the part of us that
desires control
benevolence outmans us
and slips past

SINK

So the sink is unfamiliar.
I won't make an exercise out of describing it.
There is a you.
You are incredibly hardheaded.
You have put your hands, and tools, into the sink
over a period of many years.
Here I am at the sink:
I look at myself, and it's silly to feel alienated—
better to wipe slimy stuff off the drain.

What happens at night? In the morning,
I come out of a kind of sink.
I've just seen another you in a steep village of cement playgrounds
but instead of swings, there were concrete dentist chairs.
And something else. And something else
as though you would turn me over and see bugs.
When the ship rocked,
water lashed the two-story dining room windows.
When the ship rocked, I ran
into its parking garage looking for new outfits.
Some you, I remarked to myself
as you evaded me in packed, sloped classrooms.
Or as I touched your hand
with all the force of reeling in a fish,
using my whole body,
you went to pay the check, annoyed
since—to my shame—I didn't have money.
You knew the innards of that ship. I didn't, really.
The water, all around it, spat it up.

Bright air deflects the bathroom.
Before I see myself this morning, before my inward eye
is what I guess I'll find.
I am angry at you
that you can't remember
because I know you must—
why leave me with so much?
How my head felt pressed on in the nature preserve
when we walked, hand near hand.
The specificity of blurred dirt passing under our feet.
The skin around my stomach like a belt.
All my guesses, that afternoon, about what I couldn't scrape from your
    face,
about what the weather was like in your mind,
about what other day you would rather have been walking in.
Another day, another person
whose gaze is crisp
whereas I'm a fermenting bowl.

When there isn't someone, there is sometimes someone
assuming the form of what wasn't in my day,
air leaning on me like a needy hand.
Last night, I saw them edging down my street
saying they didn't have any time for me.
Saying they had to go check on someone historical.
I went in my front door but the lights wouldn't turn on
so I put my cheek against the screen and looked out at the street.
The room stuffed with someone else's things.
I couldn't penetrate my own apartment.

I fucking refuse to stay here.
Or don't make me. Or I can't.
When I see someone at night, someone's hand refuses—mine.
In the daytime, my eyes practically bounce off my sink.
The mirror has spots of toothpaste spit.
Oh, it's you.
It's not my own life I want to organize.
I believe in where you were,
a shitty kind of faith—

There was one original experience
It was beside a lake
There was one original experience
It was an unconsummated desire
There was one original experience
It was the death of someone before I was born
There was one original experience
It was when I was menstruating and looked out a bathroom window at
    bushes

There is a you.
You are sort of beside me.
You seem to see me panic when I think my grandmother's bracelet is
    lost,
then you see me hold the bracelet.
My hand rubs a table.
My fingers roll and roll damp newsprint into tiny logs.
My eyes are open all night, up the ceiling.
High, high as they will go in the wormy dimness.

NOTES

"The end is always sudden" is a line from Arkadii Dragomoshchenko's poem "The Numerically Second Elegy," translated by Lyn Hejinian and Elena Balashova.

"Leave" borrows its form from Susan Stewart's poem "Two Brief Views of Hell."

ACKNOWLEDGEMENTS

Grateful acknowledgement is made to the editors of the following journals in which versions of these poems first appeared: *AGNI, American Poetry Review, Conduit, Crazyhorse, Denver Quarterly, Dusie, ISLE: Interdisciplinary Studies in Literature and the Environment, Kenyon Review, Lana Turner, Small House Pamphlet Series, The Canary, The Offing,* and *The Volta.* Gratitude also to *underbelly* for publishing a meditation on the revision process for this book's title poem.

Thank you to the University of South Carolina, Peter and Bonnie McCausland, and the Virginia Center for the Creative Arts for their support of this book.

Thank you to my students, colleagues, and friends. A special thanks to Kara Candito, Lindsay Bernal, Catherine Ntube, Eric Ekstrand, and Ryler Dustin for invaluable feedback on these poems.

I am grateful to have known Paul Otremba and Stanley Plumly, two poets I will never stop learning from.

Above all, love and thanks to my family. And to Sam, forever.

ABOUT THE AUTHOR

Liz Countryman teaches in the MFA program at the University of South Carolina and co-edits the annual poetry journal *Oversound*. She is the author of one previous collection, *A Forest Almost*. Her poems have appeared in *Poetry, Kenyon Review, American Poetry Review, Denver Quarterly, Lana Turner,* and *The Canary.*

Printed in the USA
CPSIA information can be obtained
at www.ICGtesting.com
LVHW041218060624
782424LV00005B/60

9 781961 209084